ESTATE PUBLICATIONS

CHIPPENHAM · CALNE
BOX · CORSHAM · MALMESBURY

C000171799

Malmesbury
4

Hullavington
5

Stanton
St Quintin
6   7
Draycot
Cerne

Kington
St Michael   Kington
8   Langley
               9

CHIPPENHAM
10   11

12

CALNE
13

Corsham
14   15
Box   Rudloe
16

Scale of street plans: 4 Inches to 1 Mile (unless otherwise stated)

━━━	Motorway	Every effort has been made to verify the accuracy of information in this book but the publishers cannot accept responsibility for expense or loss caused by an error or omission. Information that will be of assistance to the user of the maps will be welcomed.	∿ Stream / River
━━━	'A' Road / Dual		∿Lock Canal
━━━	'B' Road / Dual		→ One-way Street
━━━	Minor Road / Dual		🅿 Car Park
━━━	Track		🅲 Public Convenience
▨▨▨	Pedestrianized	The representation on these maps of a road, track or path is no evidence of the existence of a right of way.	🅸 Tourist Information
━■━	Railway / Station		✚ Place of Worship
- - -	Footpath		● Post Office

Street plans prepared and published by ESTATE PUBLICATIONS, Bridewell House, TENTERDEN, KENT.
The Publishers acknowledge the co-operation of the local authorities
of towns represented in this atlas.

OS Ordnance Survey® This product includes mapping data licensed from Ordnance Survey®
with the permission of the Controller of Her Majesty's Stationery Office.

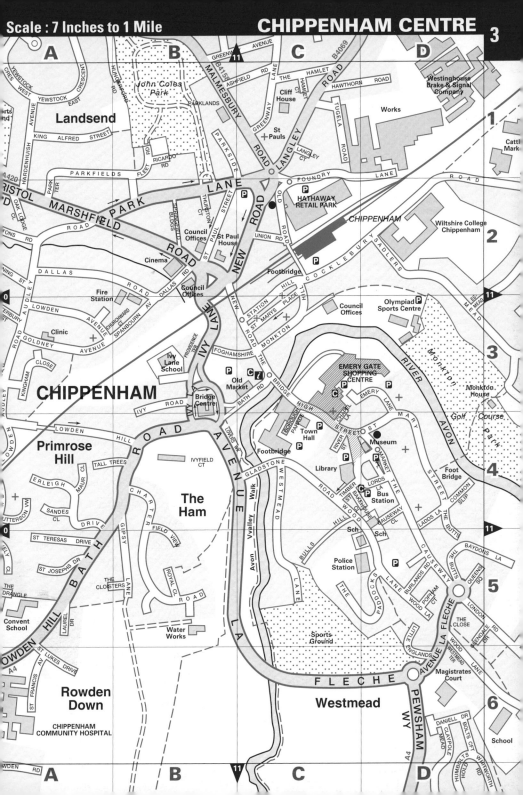

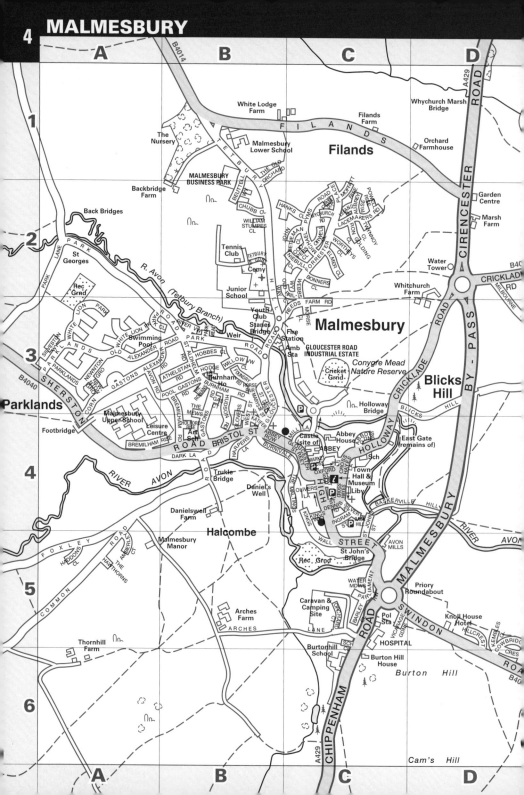

MALMESBURY

4

A   B   C   D

1

White Lodge Farm
Filands Farm
Whychurch Marsh Bridge

The Nursery
Malmesbury Lower School
Orchard Farmhouse

Filands

Backbridge Farm
MALMESBURY BUSINESS PARK
THE OLD ORCHARD

Garden Centre
Marsh Farm

2

Back Bridges
CHUBB CL
WILLIAM STUMBES CL

St Georges
Rec Grnd

Tennis Club
Cemy

Water Tower
Whitchurch Farm

Junior School

BONNERS CL

Malmesbury

Youth Club
Staines Bridge
Weir
Fire Station
Amb Sta

GLOUCESTER ROAD INDUSTRIAL ESTATE

3

Swimming Pool

HOBBES CL
WILLOW VW

Burnham Ho

Cricket Grnd

Conygre Mead Nature Reserve

Blicks Hill

Parklands

Footbridge

Malmesbury Upper School

Leisure Centre
Amb Sch
BREMILHAM RISE

THE MEWS

Holloway Bridge

East Gate (remains of)
Abbey House
Castle (site of)
ABBEY
Market
OXFORD
Town Hall & Museum
Lib
Sch

4

RIVER AVON

Trukle Bridge
Daniel's Well

DARK LA

OLIVERS LA
THE MALTINGS
ST DENNIS
INGRAM ST
KINGS

AVON MILLS

Danielswell Farm

Halcombe

Malmesbury Manor

St John's Bridge
Rec Grnd

BASKERVILLE HILL

5

FOXLEY
HADDONS CL
HAYTHORNS
THE AMBERLEY CT

WATER MDWS
PARLIAMENT

Priory Roundabout

Knoll House Hotel

Arches Farm
ARCHES

Caravan & Camping Site
BARLEY

Pol Sta

HILLCRES
KEMBLE
COWBRIDGE CRES

Thornhill Farm

COMMON

LANE
Burtonhill School
Burton Hill House

HOSPITAL

6

CHIPPENHAM

A429

Burton Hill

Cam's Hill

A   B   C   D

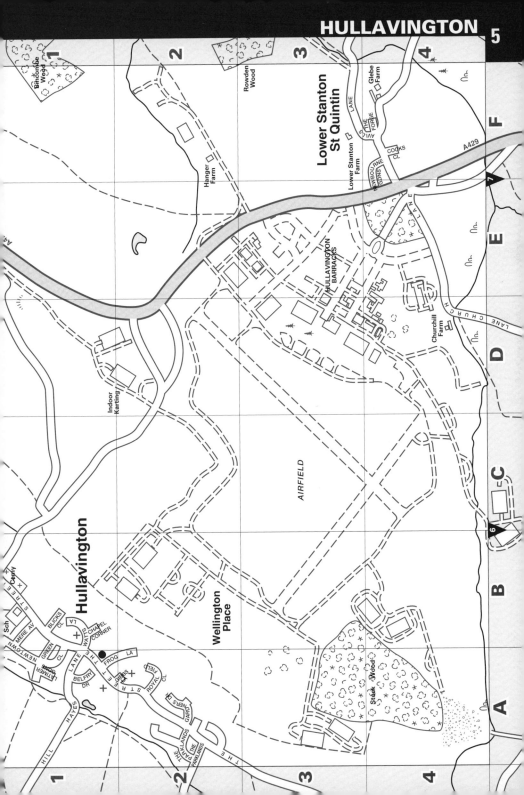

Lower Stanton
St Quintin

Hullavington

Wellington Place

AIRFIELD

Bincombe Wood

Rowden Wood

Hanger Farm

Glebe Farm

Lower Stanton Farm

HULLAVINGTON BARRACKS

Churchill Farm

Indoor Karting

Stock Wood

A429

LANE

THE FORGE

COOKS CL

NEWBOURNE GDNS

CHURCH LANE

Sch

MERE AV

BLICKS CL

NEWTOWN

GREEN CL

LATIMER RD

HAYES

HILL

Studio

BELFRY DR

FROG LA

ROYAL CL

GARD

THE PARKLANDS

STREET

WATCHAPEL CORNER

Cenny

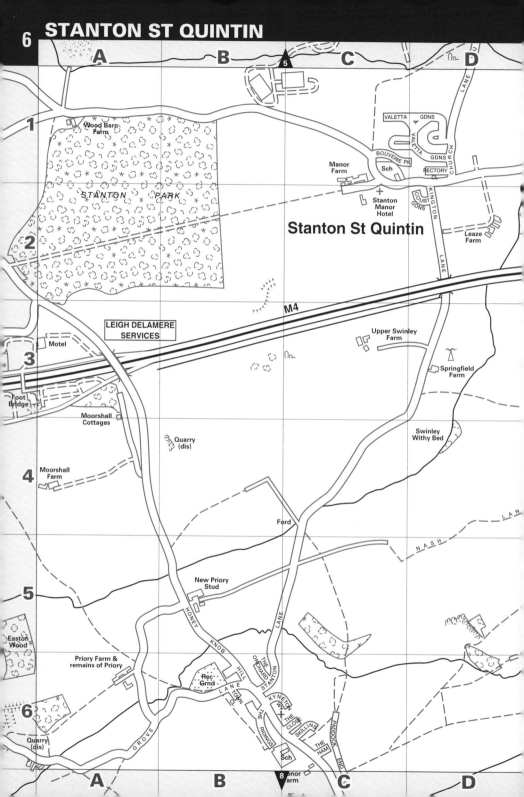

Stanton St Quintin

STANTON PARK

Wood Barn Farm

Manor Farm

Sch

VALETTA GDNS

VALETTA GDNS

BOUVERIE PK

RECTORY CL

CHURCH

KINGTON GDNS

COURT

Stanton Manor Hotel

Leaze Farm

KINGTON LANE

M4

LEIGH DELAMERE SERVICES

Motel

Foot Bridge

Moorshall Cottages

Quarry (dis)

Moorshall Farm

Upper Swinley Farm

Springfield Farm

Swinley Withy Bed

Ford

NASH LAN

New Priory Stud

Easton Wood

Priory Farm & remains of Priory

Rec Grnd

HONEY KNOB HILL

LANE

THE ORCHARD STANTON

GROVE

TOWN CL

THE RIDINGS

KYNETON WY

THE CLOSE

SKILLING

PADDOCK END

THE HAM

Sch

Manor Farm

Quarry (dis)

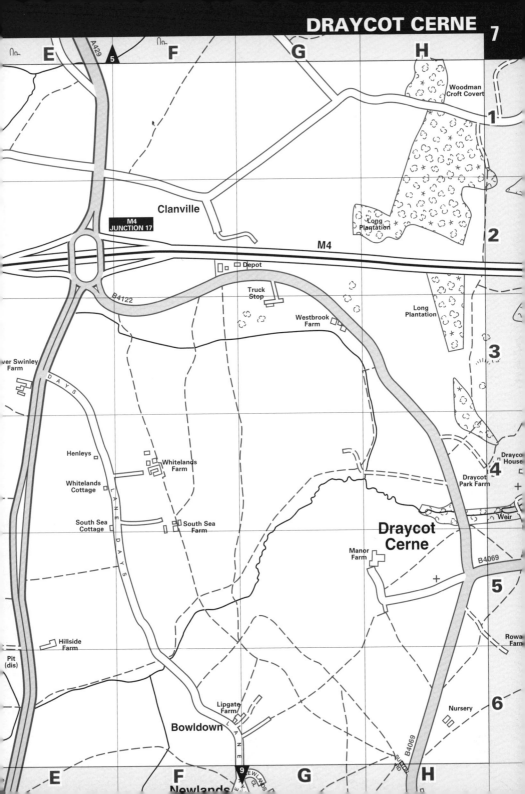

E   F   G   H

A429

5

Woodman
Croft Covert

1

Clanville

Long
Plantation

2

M4
JUNCTION 17

M4

B4122

Depot

Truck
Stop

Westbrook
Farm

Long
Plantation

River Swinley
Farm

DAYS

3

Henleys

Whitelands
Farm

Draycot
House

Whitelands
Cottage

LANE DAYS

Draycot
Park Farm

4

South Sea
Cottage

South Sea
Farm

Weir

**Draycot
Cerne**

Manor
Farm

B4069

5

Hillside
Farm

Rowa
Farm

Pit
(dis)

Lipgate
Farm

Nursery

6

Bowldown

B4069

E   F   G   H

9

Newlands

E F G H

Newlands Green

Kington Langley

1

Gate Farm

Chestnuts Farm

Greathouse

Manor House

Fairleigh Farm

Silver St

Dovey's Ter

Newlands Cl

Wayside

Middle Common

Upper Common

Lower Common

2

Sydney's Wood

Parkers La

Parkers La

The Barton

Lime Tree Farm

Nursery

Church Farm

Reservoir

Sch

Old Coppice

Reservoir

The Lawns

Long Pond Plantation

3

Stein Brook

Jacksom's Lane

Bird's Marsh

Dog Kennel Plantation

Langley House

Manor House

4

Langley Burrell

Barrow Farm

Oakhurst

Hall

Heaths Causeway

5

Maud

Common Farm

Crossing Lane

Kilverts Parsonage

Peckingell

6

St Pauls School

The Oaks

Corner

Birds Marsh Ww

Greenway Hill

Broomfield

Northwood La

Barrow Rise

Heathfield Rise

Orlands Ww

Maud Heath's Hill Causeway

Parsonage Road

Parsonage Way Industrial Estate

Cocklebury La

Upper Peckingell Farm

Lower Peckingell Farm

Oaklands

Maple Wy

Elmwood Gro

Cedar Gro

Birch Grove

Pew Road

Evans Cl

Saxby Farmer Cl

Parsonage Wy

E F G H

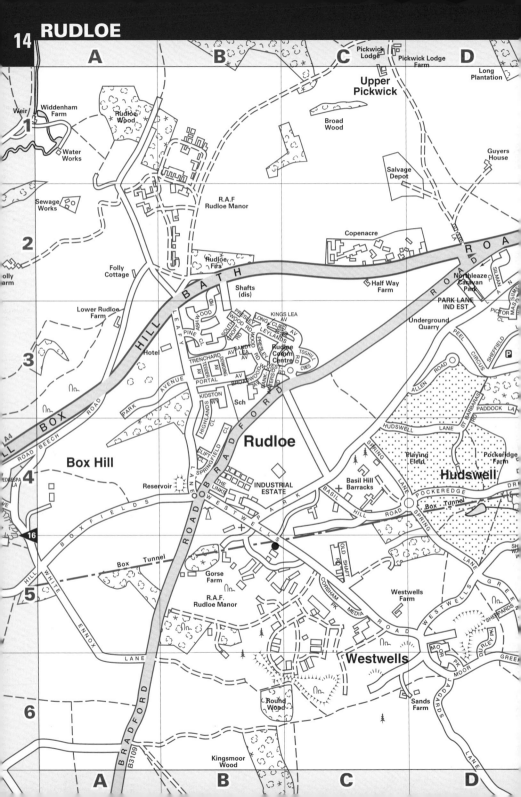

A B C D

Pickwick Lodge
Pickwick Lodge Farm

Long Plantation

Upper Pickwick

Weir
Widdenham Farm

1

Rudloe Wood

Broad Wood

Guyers House

Water Works

Salvage Depot

Sewage Works

R.A.F Rudloe Manor

Copenacre

Northleaze Caravan Park

2

Folly Farm

Folly Cottage

Rudloe Firs

Half Way Farm

PARK LANE IND EST

PICTOR CL

Lower Rudloe Farm

Shafts (dis)

KINGS LEA AV

LONG CLO AV

LEYLANDS

Underground Quarry

PEEL CIRCUS

SHEFFIELD

Hotel

ASHWOOD RD

PINE CL

WOOD RD

SOUTH DOWNING

PRESLEY

KINGS CLO

WEST CLO

TOGHIL RD

Rudloe Comm Centre

CRES

ALLEN ROAD

ST BARBARAS RD

PADDOCK LA

3

SANDY LEA AV

BANKS CLO

WATERS

HUDSWELL LANE

TRENCHARD RD

PORTAL AV

BROADWOOD AV

Rudloe

SPRING LANE

Playing Field

Pockeridge Farm

KIDSTON WY

HIGHLANDS CL

Sch

Hudswell

Box Hill

CLIFT AV

SPRINGFIELD CL

THE LINKS

INDUSTRIAL ESTATE

Basil Hill Barracks

POCKEREDGE

Box Tunnel

4

Reservoir

BRADFORD

BASIL HILL ROAD

16

BOXFIELDS

ROAD

LOWER WESTWELLS

PARK

SPRING LANE

MOOR DALE PK

SHEPPARDS

GREEN

Box   Tunnel

Gorse Farm

OLD SHAFT RD

CORSHAM MEDIA PK

Westwells Farm

WESTWELLS

SHEPPARDS

5

WHITE HILL

R.A.F. Rudloe Manor

Westwells

MOOR

JAGGARDS LANE

GREEN

ENNOX LANE

Round Wood

Sands Farm

6

BRADFORD

B3109

Kingsmoor Wood

A B C D

A - Z INDEX TO STREETS
with Postcodes

he Index includes some
ames for which there is
sufficient space on the
aps. These names are
dicated by an * and are
llowed by the nearest
djoining thoroughfare.

Street	Ref
bberd La SN11	12 D4
bberd Way SN11	13 C5
bbey Cl SN15	11 H5
bbey Row SN16	4 B4
bbots Gdns SN16	4 C4
cacia Cl SN14	10 B1
cademy Dr SN13	15 E2
ilsebury Cl SN15	11 H6
intree Dr SN14	10 A4
lexander Rd SN16	4 A3
lexander Ter SN13	15 G2
llen Rd SN13	14 D3
llington Way SN14	10 B1
ma Ter SN11	13 B5
mberley Cl SN11	12 A3
mberley Ct SN16	4 A5
nchor Rd SN11	13 C5
ndrews Cl SN14	10 C3
ngel Cl SN11	13 D5
nglesey Mead SN15	11 G6
nstey Pl SN11	11 H6
oplewood Cl SN14	10 C2
rches La SN16	4 B5
rgyle Dr SN14	8 C5
rney Cl SN13	15 F3
rnolds Mead SN13	15 F2
rundel Cl SN14	10 B3
scot Cl SN14	10 B5
she Cres SN15	9 E6
shes La SN15	9 F1
shfield Rd SN15	3 B1
shwood Rd SN13	14 B3
ubrey Rise SN16	4 C2
udley Rd SN14	3 A4
vebury Cl SN11	13 B5
vebury Rd SN14	10 B4
venue La Fleche SN15	3 B4
vils La SN14	5 F4
von Cl SN11	12 B3
von Mills SN16	4 C5
von Rd SN16	4 A3
vonmead SN15	11 F2
wdry Cl SN14	10 A3
yr Cl SN14	10 A5
zalea Cl SN11	13 C7

Street	Ref
ack Hill SN16	4 C4
ack Rd SN16	13 C6
akehouse Cl SN15	3 C4
almoral SN16	10 A3
ank Row*, Church St SN11	13 C5
ankwaters Rd SN13	14 B3
argates SN15	16 E2
arken Rd SN14	10 B1
arley Cl SN16	4 C5
arn Cl, Chippenham SN14	10 B2
arn Cl, Corsham SN13	15 E3
arn La SN13	16 E2
arn Owl Rd SN14	8 C6
arn Piece SN13	16 E2
arnes Rd SN14	8 C6
arnetts Hill SN13	16 F1
arons Mead SN14	10 B2
arrow Grn SN15	9 F6
asil Hill Rd SN14	14 C4
askerville Hill SN14	4 C4
ath Rd, Chippenham SN15	3 A5
ath Rd, Chippenham SN14	10 A5
ath Rd, Corsham SN13	14 B2
ay Cl SN11	13 D8
aydon Gro SN11	12 C3

Street	Ref
Baydons La SN15	3 D5
Bayliffes Cl SN15	11 G3
Beale Cl SN15	11 H5
Beaven Cl SN15	11 G6
Beaver Ct SN14	12 C4
Beaversbrook La SN11	12 B3
Beaversbrook Rd SN11	12 A3
Beech Rd SN13	16 F1
Beechfield Ho SN13	15 E1
Beechfield Rd SN13	15 F2
Beechwood Rd SN14	10 C2
Belfry Dr SN14	5 A1
Bellinger Cl SN15	8 D5
Bellott Dr SN13	15 E3
Bences La SN15	15 G1
Bentley Gro SN11	13 D6
Bentley La SN11	13 C7
Berkley Cl SN14	10 A3
Bethel Rd SN13	15 E3
Beuttell Way SN16	4 B2
Beverley Way SN14	10 A5
Birch Gro SN15	11 E1
Birds Marsh Vw SN15	9 E6
Bishop Cl SN15	11 F6
Bishop Rd SN11	12 B4
Blackberry Cl SN14	8 B6
Blackbridge Rd SN15	11 G2
Blackcross SN15	11 G4
Blackthorn Mews SN15	11 G6
Blackwellhams Rd SN15	11 F5
Blicks Cl SN14	5 B1
Blicks Hill SN16	4 C3
Bluebell Dr SN14	8 C5
Bluebell Gro SN11	12 C3
Bodman Cl SN15	11 F6
Bolts Cft SN15	3 D6
Bonners Cl SN16	4 C2
Boothmead SN14	10 C2
Borough Par SN15	3 C4
Boundary Rd SN15	11 G3
Bouverie Pk SN14	6 C1
Box Hill SN13	16 F1
Bradbury Cl SN15	11 H5
Bradford Rd SN13	14 A6
Braemor Rd SN11	12 A4
Brake Mead SN15	11 F3
Brakspear Dr SN13	15 F3
Bramble Dr SN14	11 G6
Bremhill Vw SN11	12 B4
Bremilham Rd SN16	4 B3
Bremilham Rise SN16	4 A4
Brewer Mead SN15	11 G5
Brewers La SN11	13 D6
Bright Cl SN15	11 G5
Brighton Way SN14	10 A4
Brinkworth Ct SN14	10 A3
Bristol Rd SN14,15	3 A2
Bristol St SN16	4 B4
Brittain Cl SN14	10 A3
Broadmead SN13	15 H4
Broadwood Av SN13	14 B3
Broken Cross SN11	13 C5
Brook Dr SN13	15 H4
Brook St SN14	10 C2
Brookway SN11	13 D5
Brookwell Cl SN15	8 D6
Broomfield SN15	9 E6
Brotherton Cl SN15	11 G5
Bruges Cl SN15	11 G3
Brunel Cl SN13	15 F2
Brunel Ct SN14	10 C4
Brunel Way SN13	16 E2
Bryans Close Rd SN11	12 C4
Buckingham Rd SN15	11 H5
Bulls Hill SN15	3 C5
Bulls La SN13	16 D2
Bumpers Farm SN14	10 B1
Bumpers Way SN14	10 A2
Burlands Rd SN15	3 D5
Burleaze SN15	10 D5
Burn Rd SN13	15 E3
Burnham Rd SN14	4 B3
Burnivale SN16	4 B4

Street	Ref
Burtons La SN13	16 D3
Buttercup Cl SN14	8 C5
Bythebrook SN14	10 B1
Campion Cl SN11	12 C3
Canal Cl SN11	13 B6
Canal Rd SN15	11 G2
Canterbury St SN15	3 A3
Carnarvon Cl SN14	10 B3
Carnegie Mews SN11	13 C5
Carnegie Rd SN11	12 D3
Carpenter Cl SN15	11 G5
Carpenters La SN14	12 A4
Carrick Cl SN15	11 G2
Cary Glen SN15	11 H6
Castle St SN11	13 B5
Castle Walk SN11	13 B5
Castlefields SN11	13 B5
Castlehaven Cl SN15	11 H5
Catterick SN14	10 A5
Causeway Cl SN15	3 D4/5
Cedar Gro SN15	11 E1
Celandine Way SN14	8 B6
Centurion Cl SN15	11 H5
Chamberlain Rd SN14	10 A2
Chandler Way SN15	11 G6
Chapel Corner SN14	5 B1
Chapel La, Chippenham SN15	3 C4
Chapel La, Corsham SN13	16 D3
Charles St SN13	15 F2
Charlieu Av SN11	13 D8
Charlwood Rd SN13	15 F3
Charter Rd SN15	3 B4
Chaveywell Ct SN13	13 B5
Cheltenham Dr SN14	10 B5
Chelwood Cl SN14	10 B5
Chepstow Cl SN14	10 A4
Cherry Tree Ct SN11	12 B3
Chester Way SN14	10 B5
Chestnut Grange SN13	15 E2
Chestnut Rd SN14	10 C2
Chevral Cl SN14	8 C6
Chilverster Hill SN11	13 A5
Chippenham Rd SN16	4 C6
Chivers Rd SN15	11 F5
Christopher Dr SN15	11 G6
Chubb Cl SN16	4 B2
Church La, Corsham SN13	16 C3
Church La, Kington Langley SN15	9 F2
Church La, Stanton St Quintin SN14	6 D1
Church Rd SN15	9 F2
Church Rise SN15	11 H5
Church St, Calne SN11	13 C5
Church St, Corsham SN13	15 G2
Church Vw SN15	8 D6
Churchill Cl SN11	13 D6
Churchill Way SN13	15 F1
Churchward Ct SN15	3 A3
Cirencester Cl SN16	4 D2
Clarence Rd SN14	10 A3
Clark Av SN11	12 C3
Claypole Mead SN15	3 D6
Cleevedale Rd SN13	15 G4
Clift Av SN15	11 F1
Clift Cl SN13	14 B4
Clifton Cl SN14	10 C2
Clover Dean SN14	10 B4
Clydesdale Rd SN13	16 D3
Cocklebury La SN15	9 F6
Cocklebury Rd SN15	3 C2
Colborne Cl SN15	11 H5
Colemans Cl SN11	13 C5
College Cl SN15	11 G2
Collen Cl SN14	10 B3
Common Cl SN16	4 A5
Common Slip SN15	3 D4
Coniston Cl SN14	10 A4
Conway Rd SN14	10 B3

Street	Ref
Cooks Cl SN14	5 F4
Coopers Cl SN16	4 C2
Cop Cft SN11	13 C5
Corfe Cres SN11	12 A4
Corn Gastons SN16	4 A3
Cornbrash Pk SN14	10 B1
Cornflower Cl SN11	12 C3
Cotswold Cl SN11	13 D6
Coulston Rd SN13	15 G1
Court Gdns SN14	6 D2
Cowbridge Cres SN16	4 D6
Cowslip Gro SN11	12 C3
Cowslip Way SN14	8 C5
Coxs Hill SN11	13 B5
Cranwell Cl SN14	10 B5
Cresswells SN13	15 F3
Cricketts La SN15	11 G5
Cricklade Rd SN16	4 C3
Cross Hayes SN16	4 C4
Cross Hayes La SN16	4 C4
Cross Keys Rd SN13	15 G1
Crossing La SN15	9 H5
Crown Cl SN15	11 G5
Cruse Cl SN14	10 A2
Culverwell Rd SN14	10 B3
Curlcroft Rd SN13	15 E5
Curlew Dr SN14	8 B6
Curzon Cl SN11	13 B5
Curzon St SN11	13 B5
Dallas Rd SN15	3 A2
Danes Cl SN15	11 G5
Daniell Dr SN15	3 D6
Danvers Mead SN15	11 H6
Danvers Rd SN13	15 E3
Darcy Cl SN15	11 G2
Dark La SN16	4 B4
Days La SN15	7 E3
Deansway SN15	11 E1
Deansway Ct SN15	8 D6
Derby Cl SN15	11 G5
Derriads Ho SN14	10 A4
Derriads La SN14	10 A4
Derriads Grn SN14	10 B3
Devizes Rd SN13	16 D3
Devon Cl SN14	10 A2
Dew Cl SN13	15 G4
Dickens Av SN13	15 F2
Dicketts Rd SN13	15 G4
Dickson Way SN15	11 F5
Dixon Way SN11	12 B4
Doctors Hill SN13	16 B3
Doncaster Cl SN14	10 A5
Dovecote Dr SN13	15 E2
Dover St SN14	10 D3
Doveys Ter SN15	9 F1
Dowding Av SN13	14 B3
Down Vw SN14	10 B3
Downham Mead SN15	11 G2
Downing St SN14	3 A2
Downland Rd SN11	13 B5
Drake Cres SN14	10 A4
Druids Cl SN11	13 A5
Dummer Way SN15	11 G5
Duncan St SN11	12 C3
Dunnet Cl SN11	12 C4
Durley Pk SN13	14 D6
Dyers Cl SN15	11 G4
Eastern Av SN15	11 G2
Easton La SN14	10 B6
Ebor Gdns SN13	13 D7
Ebor Paddock SN11	13 D7
Edinburgh Way SN13	15 E5
Edridge Cl SN15	11 G2
Edridge Pl SN13	15 E3
Elizabeth Pl SN15	11 G6
Elley Grn SN13	15 E6
Elm Cl SN15	13 D7
Elm Gro SN13	15 E2
Elm Hayes SN13	15 G4
Elmer Cl SN14	4 C2
Elmwood SN15	9 E6
Emery La SN15	3 D3
Epsom Cl SN14	10 A5
Erleigh Dr SN15	3 A4

Street	Ref
Erneston Cres SN13	15 F2
Ernle Rd SN11	12 C4
Escott Cl SN15	11 G6
Esmead SN15	3 D3
Ethelred Pl SN13	15 E2
Evans Cl SN15	11 F1
Exeter Cl SN14	10 A5
Fairfoot Cl SN14	10 B4
Fairleigh Rise SN15	9 G1
Fairway SN11	13 D8
Falcon Rd SN11	13 D5
Fallow Field Cl SN14	8 C6
Farleigh Cl SN14	10 A4
Farmer Cl SN15	11 F1
Farmhouse Dr SN15	11 G6
Farthingale Cotts SN13	15 E1
Field Vw SN15	3 B4
Filands SN16	4 B1
Fir Gro SN11	13 E7
Fishers Brook SN11	12 A1
Fitzmaurice Sq SN11	13 C5
Fitzwarren Cl SN15	11 H6
Fleet Rd SN15	3 B1
Fleetwood Cl SN13	15 E6
Foghamshire SN15	3 B3
Folkestone Cl SN14	10 B5
Foreman St SN11	13 D5
Forest La SN15	11 G5
Forrester Pl SN16	4 C2
Fortune Way SN15	11 G5
Foundry La SN15	3 C2
Foundry Rd SN16	4 B3
Fox Cl SN14	8 C6
Fox Croft Walk SN15	11 F6
Foxglove Way SN11	12 C3
Foxgrove SN14	8 B6
Foxley Rd SN14	4 A5
Fredericks Av SN14	10 A3
Frog La SN14	5 A1
Frogwell SN14	10 B3
Frogwell Pk SN14	10 B2
Fuller Av SN15	15 F3
Furzehill SN13	15 F3
Fynamore Gdns SN11	13 B6
Fynamore Pl SN11	12 C4
Gales Cl SN15	11 G2
Gardners Dr SN14	5 A2
Garth Cl SN14	8 C6
Gas Ct SN16	4 B3
Gascelyn Cl SN14	10 B3
Gastons Rd, Chippenham SN14	3 A2
Gastons Rd, Malmesbury SN16	4 B4
George Cl SN13	13 D5
George St SN11	13 D5
Gibbs La SN14	5 A2
Gipsy La SN15	3 B4
Gladstone Rd SN15	3 C4
Glebe Way SN13	15 E3
Glendale Dr SN15	3 D6
Gleneagles Cl SN15	11 G3
Gloucester Cl SN14	10 B4
Gloucester Rd SN16	4 C4
Gloucester St SN16	4 C4
Glovers Cl SN16	4 B4
Goldney Av SN15	3 A3
Goldney Ho SN15	15 F2
Goodwood Way SN14	10 A4
Granger Cl SN15	11 G6
Green Cl SN14	5 A1
Greenacres Way SN11	12 A4
Greenhill SN13	14 D5
Greenway Av SN15	11 E1
Greenway Ct SN15	9 E6
Greenway Gdns SN11	11 E1
Greenway La SN15	3 C1
Greenway Pk SN15	11 E1
Grierson Cl SN11	13 C5
Griffin Alley*, High St SN16	4 C4
Grove La SN16	4 A6
Grove Rd SN13	15 G3
Gundry Cl SN15	11 G5

17

Guthrie Cl SN11 12 D3
Guyers La SN13 14 D2

Habrels Cl SN15 11 G4
Haddons Cl SN16 4 A5
Hamilton Dr SN14 10 A5
Hamlet Ct SN15 3 C1
Hancock Cl SN15 11 H5
Hanks Cl SN16 4 B2
Hardenhuish Av SN15 3 A2
Hardenhuish La SN14 10 C1
Hardens Cl SN15 11 G5
Hardens Mead SN15 11 H4
Hardhams Rise SN13 15 F3
Hares Patch SN14 8 C5
Harford Cl SN15 11 G5
Harnish Way SN14 8 C6
Harpers La SN16 4 B4
Harris Rd SN11 12 C3
Hartham La SN13 15 F1
Hastings Rd SN13 15 G3
Hatherell Rd SN15 11 G6
Hatton Way SN13 15 E3
Hawkins Cl SN15 11 F5
Hawthorn Rd SN15 3 C1
Haydock Cl SN14 10 A5
Hayward Cl SN15 11 G5
Hazel Copse SN14 10 A4
Hazel Gro SN11 13 C6
Hazelbury Hill SN13 16 E2
Heather Way SN11 13 C7
Heathfield SN15 9 F6
Hedge Row SN15 11 G6
Hedgesparrow La SN13 16 F1
Henley La SN13 16 C4
Hereford Cl SN14 10 B5
Heron Cl SN11 13 D5
Heron Way SN14 10 A4
Hewlett Cl SN15 11 H5
Hexham Cl SN14 10 A4
High St, Box SN13 16 D3
High St, Calne SN11 13 B5
High St, Chippenham SN15 3 C3
High St, Corsham SN13 15 G1
High St, Malmesbury SN16 4 C4
Highgrove Cl SN11 13 D5
Highlands Cl SN13 14 B4
Hill Corner Rd SN15 8 D6
Hill Hayes La SN14 5 A1
Hill Rise SN15 9 E6
Hillcrest SN16 4 D5
Hillcroft SN11 13 C5
Hither Cl SN14 10 B2
Hitherspring SN13 15 F4
Hobbes Cl SN16 4 B3
Hodge La SN16 4 B3
Holford Rise SN16 4 B4
Holland Cl SN15 11 H6
Holloway SN16 4 C4
Holly Cl SN11 13 C7
Hollybush Cl SN14 8 B6
Holmes Cl SN15 11 G4
Honey Garston SN11 12 C4
Honey Knob Hill SN14 6 B5
Honeybrook Cl SN14 10 C2
Honeymead SN11 12 C4
Honeysuckle Cl, Calne SN11 12 A4
Honeysuckle Cl, Chippenham SN14 8 C5
Horse Fair SN16 4 B3
Horsebrook SN11 13 C6
Horsebrook Pk SN11 13 C6
Hudson Rd SN16 4 B3
Hudswell La SN13 14 C4
Hulbert Cl SN13 15 E3
Humbolts Hold SN15 11 F5
Hungerdown La SN14 10 B5
Hungerford Rd, Calne SN11 12 C4
Hungerford Rd, Chippenham SN15 3 A1
Huntington Way SN14 10 B5

INDUSTRIAL & RETAIL:
Bath Rd Ind Est SN14 10 C4
Beaverswork Ind Est SN11 12 C2

Bumpers Enterprise Centre SN14 10 A2
Bumpers Farm Ind Est SN14 10 B1
Corsham Media Pk SN13 14 C5
Emery Gate Shopping Centre SN15 3 C3
Fore Brooke Bsns Pk SN11 12 D2
Gloucester Rd Ind Est SN16 4 C3
Greenways Bsns Pk SN15 8 D6
Hathaway Retail Pk SN15 3 C2
Herman Miller Ind Est SN14 10 C5
Lansdowne Ct Bsns Pk SN14 10 B2
Lea Pk SN13 15 H6
Leafield Ind Est SN13 15 E5
Malmesbury Bsns Pk SN16 4 B1
Park La Ind Est SN13 14 D3
Parsonage Way Ind Est SN15 9 F6
Pheasant Bsns Pk SN14 10 C5
Porte Marsh Ind Est SN11 12 D2
Station Rd Ind Est SN11 13 B6
The Leys Bsns Pk SN13 16 D3
Westpoint Bsns Pk SN14 10 A2

Ingram St SN14 4 C4
Ivy Fld SN13 15 G1
Ivy La SN15 3 B4
Ivy Rd SN15 3 B4
Ivyfield Ct SN15 3 B4

Jacksom's La SN15 8 D4
Jaggards La SN13 14 D6
James Cl SN15 11 G6
Jargeau Ct SN13 15 G3
Jasmine Cl SN11 13 C6
John Betjeman Cl SN16 4 C2
Jordon Cl SN15 11 G5

Katifer La SN16 4 B4
Keevil Av SN11 13 A5
Kelso Ct SN14 10 B5
Kembles Cl SN16 4 D5
Kempton Park Ct SN14 10 A4
Kensington Way SN14 10 A3
Kent Cl SN14 10 B4
Kerry Cres SN11 13 C5
Kidston Way SN13 14 B3
Kilverts Cl SN14 10 B4
King Alfred St SN15 3 A1
King Henry Dr SN15 11 G6
Kingham Cl SN14 3 A3
Kings Av, Chippenham SN14 10 A4
Kings Av, Corsham SN13 15 F1
Kings Lea Av SN13 14 B3
Kings Walk SN16 4 C4
Kings Wall SN16 4 C4
Kingsbury St SN11 13 C5
Kingsley Rd SN14 10 C4
Kington La SN14 6 D2
Kirby Rd SN13 15 F2
Knight Cl SN15 11 G6
Kyneton Way SN14 6 B6

Lacemakers Rd SN14 4 C2
Lackham Circus SN14 10 C4
Lacock Rd SN13 15 G3
Ladbrook La SN15 11 H5
Ladds La SN15 3 D4
Lady Coventry Rd SN15 11 G3
Ladyfield Rd SN14 10 C4
Laines Head SN15 8 D6
Lamberts SN14 10 B2
Langley Ct SN15 3 C1
Langley Rd SN15 3 C1

Lanhill Vw SN14 8 C6
Lansdown Gro SN15 11 E1
Lansdowne Cl SN11 12 B4
Lapwing Cres SN14 8 C6
Larkham Rise SN15 11 F4
Latimer Gdns SN14 5 A1
Laurel Dr SN15 3 A5
Lavender Dr SN11 13 C6
Leafield Rd SN13 15 E6
Leafield Way SN13 15 E4
Leafy La SN13 14 B3
Legate Cl SN15 11 H5
Leland Cl SN16 4 C2
Lenton Cl SN14 10 A3
Leylands Rd SN13 14 B3
Lickhill Rd SN11 12 B3
Light Cl SN13 15 G1
Lilac Way SN11 13 C6
Lime Tree Cl SN11 13 A5
Linden Cl SN13 13 C6
Lingfield Cl SN14 10 A5
Little Down SN14 10 C3
Little Englands SN15 3 D5
Littlecote Rd SN14 10 A3
Littlemead SN13 16 B3
Lockside SN15 11 F5
Lockswell Cl SN15 11 H6
Lodge Cl SN11 13 A5
Lodge Rd SN15 11 G5
Londale Dr SN15 11 F4
London Rd, Calne SN11 13 C6
London Rd, Chippenham SN15 3 D5
London Rd, Corsham SN13 16 D2
Long Cl SN15 11 G4
Long Close Av SN13 14 B3
Long Ridings SN15 8 D6
Longbarrow Rd SN11 13 A5
Longsplatt SN13 16 C4
Longstone SN14 10 B1
Lords La SN15 3 D4
Lords Mead SN14 10 B2
Love La SN13 16 F1
Lovers Walk SN15 3 B4
Low La SN11 13 D6
Lowden SN14,15 3 A4
Lowden Av SN15 3 A3
Lowden Hill SN15 3 A4
Lower Common SN15 9 F1
Lower Kingsdown Rd SN13 16 B4
Loyalty St SN14 3 A3
Luckett Way SN11 12 C4
Ludlow Cl SN15 11 G5
Ludmead Rd SN13 15 G4
Lydiard Rd SN14 10 B4
Lypiatt Mead SN15 3 A5
Lypiatt Rd SN13 15 G4
Lysley Cl SN15 11 G5
Lytham Cl SN15 11 G5

Macaulay Sq SN11 13 C5
Magnolia Rise SN11 13 C6
Maitland Cl SN15 11 H5
Mallard Cl SN11 13 D5
Malmesbury By-Pass SN16 4 C5
Malmesbury Rd SN15 3 B1
Manor Rd, Chippenham SN14 10 B2
Manor Rd, Corsham SN13 15 F1
Maple Cl SN15 13 C7
Maple Way SN15 9 E6
Marden Way SN11 13 B6
Market Cross SN16 4 C4
Market Hill SN11 13 B5
Market La SN16 4 C4
Market Pl, Chippenham SN15 3 D4
Market Pl, Corsham SN13 16 D3
Marlborough Ct SN14 10 C3
Marshall St SN14 10 D3
Marshfield Rd SN15 3 A2
Martin Way SN11 13 D5
Martins Cl SN15 11 G2
Masons Way SN13 14 D3
Massey Cl SN15 11 F5
Matford Hill SN15 11 G2
Maundrell Rd SN11 12 C2

Maur Cl SN15 3 A4
Mayo Cl SN13 15 E2
Meadland SN13 15 E2
Meadow Cl SN14 10 B3
Meadow Vw SN11 13 D8
Meadowsweet Dr SN11 12 A4
Melksham Rd SN15 11 G3
Mere Av SN14 5 B1
Meriton Av SN13 15 G2
Methuen Way SN13 15 F1
Michael Pyms Rd SN16 4 C2
Middle Common SN15 9 E2
Middlewick La SN13 15 E1
Milbourne La SN16 4 D2
Milestone Way SN13 8 D6
Milford Way SN15 11 F6
Mill La, Corsham SN13 16 C2
Mill La, Malmesbury SN16 4 C4
Mill St SN11 13 C5
Millard Cl SN15 11 G6
Minster Way SN14 10 B5
Moffatt Rise SN16 4 C2
Monks La SN13 15 H6
Monks Way SN15 11 H6
Monkton Hill SN15 3 C3
Montague Cl SN15 11 G2
Moor Barton SN13 15 E6
Moor Grn SN13 14 D6
Moor Pk SN13 14 D5
Moorlands SN15 9 F6
Moors Cl SN15 8 D2
Morse Cl, Chippenham SN15 11 F6
Morse Cl, Malmesbury SN16 4 C4
Moss Mead SN14 10 A2
Mount Pleasant SN14 10 B1
Mulberry Cl SN14 10 B1
Murrayfield SN15 11 E1

Nash La SN14 6 D5
Neale Ct SN13 15 F2
Neeld Cres SN14 10 C2
Nestleton Cl SN11 13 C6
Neston Cres SN13 15 E6
New Rd, Calne SN11 13 C5
New Rd, Chippenham SN15 3 C2
Newall Tuck Rd SN15 11 G3
Newbourne Gdns SN14 5 E4
Newbury Av SN11 12 A4
Newbury Dr SN14 10 B5
Newcroft Cl SN15 12 B3
Newcroft Rd SN11 12 B4
Newlands Cl SN15 9 F1
Newlands Rd SN13 15 G2
Newmarket Cl SN14 10 A4
Newnton Gro SN16 4 A3
Newton Abbot Cl SN14 10 A5
Newtown SN14 5 A1
Niebull Cl SN16 4 C2
Norman Cl SN15 11 H6
North End SN11 12 B4
North St SN11 12 B4
Northcote SN11 12 B4
Northfields SN11 12 B4
Northway SN11 12 B4
Northwood SN15 9 E6
Noyes Cl SN14 10 A2
Nursery Gdns SN13 15 G3

Oldbury Prior SN11 13 D
Oldbury Way SN11 13 B
Oliver Av SN13 15 F
Olivers La SN16 4 C
Orchard Cl SN11 13 C
Orchard Cres SN11 10 C
Orchard Ct SN16 4 C
Orchard Rd, Chippenham SN14 10 C
Orchard Rd, Corsham SN13 15 G
Orwell Cl SN16 4 C
Oxford Rd SN11 13 C
Oxford St SN16 4 C

Paddock End SN14 6 C
Paddock La SN13 14 D
Page Cl, Calne SN11 13 D
Page Cl, Chippenham SN14 10 B
Palmer St SN14 10 D
Park Av, Chippenham SN14 10 C
Park Av, Corsham SN13 14 A
Park Cl, Calne SN11 13 D
Park Cl, Malmesbury SN16 4 A
Park La, Chippenham SN15 3 E
Park La, Corsham SN13 14 E
Park La, Malmesbury SN16 4 A
Park Mead SN16 4 E
Park Rd SN16 4 A
Park Ter SN15 3 A
Parkers La SN15 9 E
Parkfields SN15 3 A
Parklands, Chippenham SN15 3 E
Parklands, Malmesbury SN16 4 A
Parkside SN15 3 E
Parliament Row SN16 4 C
Parliament St SN14 10 C
Parsonage Way SN15 9 F
Partridge Cl, Chippenham SN14 8 C
Partridge Cl, Corsham SN13 15 E
Patchway SN14 10 C
Patford St SN11 13 E
Paul St SN13 15 F
Pavely Cl SN15 3 A
Payne Cl SN15 11 F
Peel Circus SN14 14 C
Pembroke Rd SN15 11 H
Penleigh Cl SN13 15 F
Penn Hill Rd SN14 8 C
Penny La SN15 11 G
Penny Royal Cl SN11 12 A
Pew Hill SN15 9 F
Pewsham Lock SN15 11 F
Pewsham Way SN15 11 G
Pheasant Cl SN14 10 A
Phelps Par SN11 13 C
Phillips Cl SN14 10 A
Picketleaze SN14 10 B
Pickwick Cl SN13 15 E
Pickwick Rd SN13 15 E
Pictor Cl SN15 14 D
Pine Cl SN13 14 B
Pinfield La SN15 11 G
Pinhills SN11 13 B
Pippin Row SN11 13 C
Pipsmore Rd SN14 10 B
Pitts Cft SN13 15 E
Plantation Rd SN14 10 A
Plough Corner SN15 8 D
Plough La SN15 8 D
Plumpton Cl SN14 10 A
Pockeredge Dr SN13 14 D
Pockeridge Rd SN13 15 E
Pool Gastons Rd SN16 4 A
Pool Grn SN13 15 E
Popham Ct SN15 3 D
Poppy Cl SN11 12 A
Portal Av SN13 15 F
Porte Marsh Rd SN11 12 C
Portland Way SN11 13 C
Portway SN14 10 C
Post Office La SN13 15 G

Street	Postcode	Ref
otley La	SN13	15 E4
ound Mead	SN13	15 F4
ound Pill	SN13	15 G3
owell Rise	SN16	4 C2
oynder Rd	SN13	15 E2
esley Wood Rd SN13		14 B3
iestley Gro	SN11	13 D6
imrose La	SN11	12 C3
imrose Way	SN13	8 C6
ince Charles Dr SN11		13 D5
iory New Rd	SN13	15 F1
iory St	SN13	15 F1
ospect, Corsham	SN13	15 G4
ospect, Kingsdown	SN13	16 B4
ovidence La	SN13	15 F2
ovidence Ter	SN15	3 B3
ovis Mead	SN15	11 H6
urbeck Pl	SN11	13 D6
urleigh Rd	SN13	15 E2
uarr Barton	SN13	13 B5
uarry Hill	SN13	16 E2
uarrydale Cl	SN13	13 C6
ueens Av	SN13	15 F1
ueens Cres	SN14	10 B4
ueens Sq, Chippenham	SN15	3 D5
ueens Sq, Corsham	SN13	16 D3
uemerford	SN11	13 D7
andall Ct	SN13	15 E2
ay Cl	SN15	11 G5
ectory Cl	SN14	6 D1
edland	SN14	10 C2
edman Rd	SN11	12 C2
edwing Av	SN14	8 C6
eeds Farm Rd	SN16	4 C3
icardo Rd	SN14	3 B1
ichmond Rd	SN11	12 A4
dgemead	SN11	12 B3
idings Mead	SN15	8 D6
ipon	SN14	10 B5
iver St	SN15	3 C4
iver Vw	SN16	4 B3
iverside	SN11	13 D7
iverside Dr	SN15	11 G3
obins Cl	SN14	8 C6
ochdale Av	SN11	12 C3
oman Way	SN15	11 H5
on Rolding Cl	SN16	4 C2
ookery Pk	SN11	13 D8
ooks Nest Cl	SN15	11 G6
osemary Cl	SN11	12 A4
ough St	SN13	15 F6
ound Ho	SN11	13 D7
owan Cotts	SN13	15 E1
owden Hill	SN15	3 A6
owden La	SN15	10 C5
owden Rd	SN15	10 D4
owe Mead	SN15	11 F5
oyal Cl	SN15	3 B5
oyal Field Cl	SN14	5 A2
umble Dene	SN15	11 F5
van Av	SN14	10 B3

Street	Postcode	Ref
St Mary St	SN15	3 D4
St Marys La	SN16	4 B3
St Marys Pl	SN13	3 C3
St Marys St	SN16	4 B3
St Mellion Cl	SN15	11 G3
St Nicholas Cl	SN11	12 D4
St Paul St	SN15	3 B2
St Peters Cl	SN15	10 C4
St Teresas Dr	SN15	3 A5
Salisbury Cl	SN14	10 B4
Saltersford La	SN14	10 B5
Sand Pit Rd	SN11	12 D3
Sandes Cl	SN15	3 A4
Sandown Dr	SN14	10 A5
Sandpiper Gdns	SN14	8 B6
Sandy Lea Av	SN13	14 B3
Sandy Ridge	SN11	13 D6
Sarum Rd	SN14	10 B4
Sarum Way	SN11	13 A5
Saunders Gro	SN13	15 E3
Savernake Dr	SN11	13 A5
Savernake Rd	SN13	15 E4
Saxby Rd	SN15	9 F6
Saxon St	SN14	10 C2
School Cl	SN16	4 C5
School Walk	SN14	10 B3
Sedgefield Way	SN14	10 A4
Selions Cl	SN14	8 C6
Seymour Rd	SN15	11 G2
Shearwater Way	SN13	14 D5
Sheepscroft	SN14	8 C6
Sheffield La	SN11	13 D3
Shelburne Rd	SN11	13 C6
Sheldon Rd	SN14	10 C3
Sheppard Cl	SN15	11 G6
Sheppards	SN14	14 D5
Sherrington Mead	SN15	11 H6
Sherston Rd	SN16	4 A3
Silbury Cl	SN14	10 B5
Silbury Rd	SN11	13 B5
Silman Cl	SN13	14 D2
Silver St, Calne	SN11	13 B8
Silver St, Chippenham	SN15	9 F1
Silver St, Corsham	SN13	15 H5
Silver St, Malmesbury	SN16	4 C4
Silveston Way	SN16	4 A3
Skillins	SN14	6 C6
Smiths Yd	SN13	15 G2
Sorrel Dr	SN14	8 C5
South Av	SN13	15 G3
South Pl, Calne	SN11	13 C6
South Pl, Corsham	SN13	15 F3
South St	SN13	15 G3
Southcroft Rd	SN13	14 B3
Southerwicks	SN13	15 F3
Southmead	SN14	10 C4
Southwell Cl	SN14	10 B5
Spackman La	SN15	15 E3
Spanbourn Av	SN15	3 B3
Spinney	SN14	10 B4
Spring Gdns	SN13	15 G2
Spring La	SN13	14 C4
Springfield Bldgs	SN15	3 B2
Springfield Cl	SN13	14 B4
Springfield Dr	SN11	12 A4
Stainers Way	SN14	8 B6
Stanier Rd	SN11	12 C2
Stanley La	SN15	11 H5
Stanton La	SN14	6 B6
Stapleford Cl	SN11	11 F6
Station Hill	SN15	3 C3
Station Rd, Calne	SN11	13 B6
Station Rd, Corsham	SN13	15 G3
Stewart Cl	SN15	11 G6
Stockley La	SN11	13 D8
Stockwood Rd	SN14	10 C4
Stokes Cft	SN11	12 C4
Stokes Rd	SN13	15 G3

Street	Postcode	Ref
Stonelea Cl	SN14	10 C3
Stubbs La	SN14	8 B2
Sumsions Dr	SN13	14 D2
Sunningdale Cl	SN15	11 F3
Sutherland Cres	SN14	8 C5
Sutton Rd	SN15	7 H6
Swaddon St	SN11	12 C4
Swan Rd	SN13	15 E2
Swanborough Cl	SN15	11 G6
Swayne Cl	SN15	11 F5
Swindon Rd	SN16	4 C5
Sydney Wood Ct	SN14	10 D3
Syon Cl	SN13	15 E3
Tall Trees	SN15	3 A4
Tamarisk Cl	SN11	13 C7
Tanner Cl	SN11	11 G5
Tasker Cl	SN13	15 E3
Taunton Cl	SN14	10 A5
Tavinor Dr	SN14	11 F6
Tedder Av	SN13	14 B3
Tellcroft Cl	SN13	15 G4
Tern Cl	SN11	13 D5
Tetbury Hill	SN16	4 B1
Tetbury Hill Gdns	SN16	4 B2
Thatcham Cl	SN11	12 A4
The Barton	SN15	9 E2
The Bassetts	SN13	16 D2
The Battens	SN14	10 B1
The Bridge	SN15	3 C3
The Brownings	SN13	16 D3
The Butts	SN15	3 D4/5
The Causeway	SN15	3 D4
The Cleeve	SN13	15 G4
The Cloisters	SN15	3 A5
The Close, Chippenham	SN15	3 D5
The Close, Kington St Michael	SN14	6 C6
The Firs	SN14	10 B4
The Forge	SN14	5 F4
The Glebe	SN11	13 C5
The Green	SN11	13 C6
The Gullet	SN13	16 F1
The Ham	SN14	6 C6
The Hamlet	SN15	3 C1
The Hawthorns	SN16	4 A5
The Kilns	SN11	12 D4
The Knapp	SN11	13 C5
The Knowle, Calne	SN11	13 D8
The Knowle, Corsham	SN13	15 F3
The Laggar	SN13	15 F1
The Ley	SN13	16 D3
The Links	SN13	14 B4
The Maltings	SN16	4 C4
The Mews	SN14	4 B3
The Oaks	SN15	9 E6
The Old Orchard	SN16	4 B1
The Orangery	SN13	15 E1
The Orchard	SN14	6 B6
The Paddocks	SN15	3 C5
The Parklands	SN14	5 A2
The Pippin	SN13	15 C5
The Poplars	SN14	10 B1
The Precinct	SN15	15 G2
The Quadrangle	SN15	3 A5
The Quarry	SN11	13 C6
The Ridings	SN14	6 B6
The Rise	SN11	13 C8
The Rowans	SN16	4 B3
The Slades	SN11	12 D4
The Square	SN11	13 B5
The Stables	SN13	15 E1
The Strand	SN11	13 B5
The Street	SN14	5 A2
The Tinings	SN15	11 G2
The Turnpike	SN15	11 H5
The Tynings	SN13	15 G3
The Wharf, Calne	SN11	13 C5

Street	Postcode	Ref
The Wharf, Corsham	SN13	16 D2
The Willows	SN11	13 F8
The Wynd	SN14	10 B5
Thirsk Cl	SN14	10 B5
Thomas Ct	SN11	13 C6
Thomas Mead	SN15	11 F6
Thurston Cl	SN15	3 B2
Timber St	SN15	3 C4
Toghill Cres	SN13	14 C3
Torr Cl	SN14	8 C6
Towcester Cl	SN14	10 A5
Town Cl	SN14	6 B6
Townsend Pl	SN14	10 A2
Trenchard Av	SN13	14 B3
Trenchard Cl	SN14	10 B4
Trimbrells Pl	SN15	10 C4
Trinity Pk	SN11	13 D7
Tropenell Cl	SN13	15 E3
Truro Walk	SN14	10 A4
Tudor Cl	SN15	11 H6
Tugela Rd	SN15	3 C1
Tupman Rd	SN13	15 F2
Turnberry Cl	SN15	11 G3
Turpin Way	SN11	10 A3
Twickenham Way	SN15	11 E1
Twynnoy Cl	SN16	4 C2
Tyning Pk	SN11	13 C7
Union Rd	SN15	3 C2
Unity St	SN14	10 D3
Upper Common	SN15	9 E2
Upper Farm Barns	SN14	8 C6
Upper Ley	SN13	15 E5
Upper Potley	SN13	15 E5
Utterson Vw	SN15	3 A4
Valens Ter	SN13	16 D2
Valetta Gdns	SN14	6 C1
Valley Rd	SN13	15 E2
Valley Vw	SN11	13 B6
Vicarage Cl	SN11	13 C5
Vicarage Gdns	SN16	4 C5
Victoria Ter	SN11	12 B4
Villiers Cl	SN15	11 G3
Vincients Rd	SN14	10 A2
Vine Ct	SN13	16 E2
Walter Sutton Cl	SN11	13 A5
Wansdyke Dr	SN11	13 B5
Wardour Rd	SN14	10 B4
Warren Cres	SN11	12 C4
Warwick Cl	SN14	10 A5
Wastfield	SN13	15 F4
Water Mdws	SN16	4 C5
Water Mint Way	SN11	12 A4
Waters Edge	SN15	11 F5
Watts La	SN14	5 B1
Waverley Ct	SN13	15 G3
Wayside	SN15	9 F1
Weavern Ct	SN14	10 B3
Weavers Cl, Chippenham	SN14	10 A3
Weavers Cl, Malmesbury	SN16	4 C2
Webb Cl	SN15	11 F5
Webbington Rd	SN15	11 F5
Webbs Way	SN16	4 C2
Wedmore Av	SN15	10 D1
Weir Hayes Av	SN13	14 B3
Weller Rd	SN13	15 F2
Wells Cl	SN14	10 B5
Wenhill Heights	SN11	13 B6
Wenhill La	SN11	13 A6
Wentworth Cl	SN15	11 G3
Wessex Cl	SN11	13 D5
Wessex Rd	SN14	10 C2
Wessington Av	SN11	13 D7
Wessington Cl	SN11	13 D7
Wessington Pk	SN11	13 D6
West Cepen Way	SN14	10 A4
West Dr	SN15	15 E2
West Park Rd	SN13	15 E2

Street	Postcode	Ref
West St	SN16	4 B4
Westbrook Cl	SN14	10 B3
Westcroft	SN14	10 B5
Westcroft Cl	SN14	10 B5
Westerham Walk	SN11	13 D6
Westerleigh Cl	SN14	10 C4
Westmead La	SN15	3 C4
Westmead Ter	SN15	3 D6
Westminster Gdns	SN14	10 C3
Westwells	SN13	14 B4
Westwells Rd	SN13	14 B4
Westwood Rd	SN13	14 B3
Wetherby	SN14	10 B5
White Ennox La	SN13	14 A5
White Horse Way	SN11	13 C7
White Lion Pk	SN16	4 A3
Whitehall Gdns	SN11	13 B5
Whittle Cl	SN14	10 B3
Whitworth Rd	SN15	3 D6
Wicks Dr	SN15	11 G5
William St	SN11	13 B5
William Stumpes Cl	SN16	4 B2
Williams Gro	SN13	15 G3
Willis Cl	SN15	11 G6
Willow Gro	SN15	9 E6
Willow View Cl	SN16	4 B3
Willowbank	SN14	8 B6
Winchester Cl	SN14	10 B4
Windlass Way	SN15	11 F5
Windsor Cl	SN14	10 B4
Wintergreen	SN11	12 A4
Wishart Way	SN15	11 F5
Wolverton Cl	SN14	10 A4
Wood La, Chippenham	SN15	3 C4
Wood La, Chippenham	SN15	3 D5
Wood St	SN11	13 C5
Woodborough Rd	SN13	15 H4
Woodhill Av	SN11	12 D4
Woodhill Rise	SN11	12 D4
Woodland Pk	SN11	13 C6
Woodlands	SN13	15 E1
Woodlands Rd	SN14	10 C3
Woodpecker Mews	SN14	8 C6
Woodroffe Sq	SN11	13 D5
Woodsage Way	SN11	12 A4
Wormcliffe La	SN13	16 A4
Wortheys Cl	SN14	4 C2
Wychurch Rd	SN16	4 C2
Wyndham Cl	SN15	11 G2
Wyvern Av	SN11	13 D5
Yew Tree Cl	SN11	13 A5
Yewstock Cres East	SN15	3 A1
Yewstock Cres West	SN15	3 A1
Yockney Cl	SN13	15 E3
York Cl, Chippenham	SN14	10 B4
York Cl, Corsham	SN13	15 F1

For an up-to-date publication list and latest prices visit our web site at

www.estate-publications.co.uk

Use the search facility to find the village, town or city you require.

Local Red Books (selection of)

Ashford & Tenterden	Lancaster & Morecambe
Barnstaple & Ilfracombe	Lincoln
Basildon & Billericay	Macclesfield & Wilmslow
Basingstoke & Andover	Maidstone
Bath & Bradford-upon-Avon	Medway & Gillingham
Bedford	Newport & Chepstow
Brentwood	Northampton
Bromley (London Borough)	Norwich
Burton-upon-Trent & Swadlincote	Nuneaton & Bedworth
Cambridge	Oxford & Abingdon
Chelmsford, Braintree & Maldon	Peterborough
Chester	Plymouth, Saltash & Torpoint
Chesterfield	Reading & Henley-on-Thames
Chichester & Bognor Regis	Redditch & Bromsgrove
Colchester & Clacton	Rugby
Crewe	Salisbury, Amesbury & Wilton
Eastbourne, Bexhill, Seaford & Newhaven	Sevenoaks
Exeter & Exmouth	Southend-on-Sea
Fareham & Gosport	Stafford
Folkestone, Dover, Deal & Romney Marsh	Swindon
Gloucester & Cheltenham	Telford
Gravesend & Dartford	Tunbridge Wells & Tonbridge
Great Yarmouth & Lowestoft	Warwick & Royal Leamington Spa
Hereford	Weston-super-Mare & Clevedon
Ipswich & Felixstowe	Winchester
Kidderminster	Wolverhampton (Sheet Map)
Kingston-upon-Hull	York

Super Red Books

Birmingham (Colour)
Bournemouth
Brighton
Bristol
Cardiff
Coventry
Derby
Edinburgh
Glasgow
Leicester
Nottingham
Portsmouth
Southampton (Colour)
Stoke-on-Trent
Swansea

County Red Books

Bedfordshire	Lincolnshire
Berkshire	Norfolk
Buckinghamshire	Northamptonshire
Cambridgeshire	Nottinghamshire
Cheshire	Oxfordshire
Cornwall	Shropshire
Derbyshire	Somerset
Devon	Staffordshire
Dorset	Suffolk
Essex	Surrey
Gloucestershire	Sussex (East)
Hampshire	Sussex (West)
Herefordshire	Warwickshire
Kent	Wiltshire
Leicestershire & Rutland	Worcestershire

Estate Publications, Bridewell House, Tenterden, Kent, TN30 6EP
Tel: 01580 764225 Fax: 01580 763720